THE
BLUFFER'S GUIDE
TO
WOMEN

MARINA MURATORE

D1393104

RR

RAVETTE PUBLISHING

Published by Ravette Publishing Limited
P.O. Box 296
Horsham
West Sussex RH13 8FH

Telephone: (01403) 711443
Fax: (01403) 711554

Series Editor – Anne Tauté

Cover design – Jim Wire, Quantum
Printing & binding – Cox & Wyman Ltd.
Production – Oval Projects Ltd.

The Bluffer's Guides™ series is based
on an original idea by Peter Wolfe.

The Bluffer's Guides™, Bluffer's™
and Bluff Your Way™ are Trademarks.

An Oval Project
for Ravette Publishing.

For their invaluable contributions to
this guide, acknowledgement and
grateful thanks are given to:

Cathy Douglas, Sally Horton,
Eva Lipniaka, Catriona Scott,
Pauline Rozendaal, Jill Howell,
Drew Launay and Antony Mason.

CONTENTS

THE KEY TO UNDERSTANDING WOMEN

There isn't one.

From the beginning of time, women have induced ecstasy, provoked murder, caused wars and left indelible evidence on countless collars – all the while proclaiming ignorance of what the fuss is about.

Women don't understand other women, and don't even understand themselves, while men, who claim to know everything, have for millions of years been happy to admit that they cannot understand women. As Thackeray put it: "When I say that I know women, I mean I know that I don't know them. Every single woman I ever knew is a puzzle to me, as, I have no doubt, she is to herself."

The fact is that both sexes rather like to perpetuate this belief. Women enjoy the feeling of being all-knowing but unknowable: it gives them a rare edge. Men like to absolve themselves of the need to work it out – without a sense of personal failure. If *no* man can understand women, it's not his fault if he doesn't.

When discussing women, therefore, always bear in mind that no-one has the faintest idea what they are talking about, and the person who wins the argument on the subject can only be a bluffer.

THE ESSENTIAL DIFFERENCE

Men and women are now held to be equal, but they are not the same. This has to be acknowledged, even by die-hard males who defiantly see women as flawed versions of themselves, and by women in boiler suits who see men as superfluous.

While men believe themselves to be ordinary, common or garden members of the human race (well, never that ordinary, of course) women know they are different, something apart. They have a perspective on the world that is uniquely their own.

Body Design

Whatever the standpoint, no-one can dispute that men and women are built to totally different specifications:

a) Women are rounder, softer to the touch and smell a lot better.

b) Women's most essential equipment is kept tidily within the engine housing. Men have an exterior telescopic urinary device that seems to have a mind of its own.

c) Women's bodies naturally contain more fat – 25% of their body weight, compared with 12½% in men's. This has advantages as insurance against cold and as an aid to buoyancy.

d) Unlike men, women have useful breasts that can produce milk when called upon and store fat for times of famine. In fact, only one third of the breast is devoted to the function of lactation, the rest is food-storage. As it happens, big breasts do not necessarily mean successful breast-feeding because they can get clogged with fat glands which obstructs milk-production. It is a well-known maxim of the farmyard that you shouldn't buy a fat cow.

e) Women are equipped with a magical component that transforms men's impetuous spermatozoa into human beings.

The XX Factor

Every human has a string of 23 pairs of chromosomes (the genetic markers that carry hereditary features such as blue eyes, knock knees and preferred choice of cocktail). Until the seventh week after conception, the foetus is gender-dormant but at this point, if the child is to be male, the solitary 'Y' in its XY pair of sex chromosomes kicks in – and the production of another little lord and master is set in motion. If the child is to be a female, its XX sex chromosome ensures that the foetus continues blithely on its female path.

The female, therefore, can be seen as what, in computer technology, is termed the 'default' programme – that is, the one the machine is coded to use unless instructed otherwise. So much for the story of Creation: clearly Eve was not made from Adam's rib, but Adam simply a chip off the eternal Eve.

Male bluffers could try arguing that the creative input of the male Y chromosome represents something positive and clever in itself. However, females might respond that it can equally well be viewed as an afterthought, and that the fact that maleness is only accounted for by 1/46th of a person's heredity makes it very small beer. Or in Zsa-Zsa Gabor's words: "Macho doesn't mean mucho."

The XX factor has a number of advantages over the XY:

- Women are less prone to colour blindness.
- Women have a more acute sense of hearing, taste, smell and touch.
- Women's eyes adjust faster, so they can see better in the dark, useful for slamming the alarm clock button before dawn.

The XX chromosome also carries a socialising gene, the 'sugar and spice and all things nice' of the nursery rhyme. The male lacks this ready-made factor. He has to learn to be nice.

Doctors are likely to tell you that it is hard enough identifying genes that cause major illnesses, let alone something as vague and fancy as socialising genes. But you should not let science get in the way of a good idea.

Blame Oestrogen

It is the sex hormone oestrogen that effectively makes a woman a woman. Produced chiefly in her ovaries, oestrogen brings about a woman's metamorphosis at puberty from beanbag to egg-timer, activates her womb and controls her moon-like cycle. It is the decline in oestrogen production in late middle age that sets off the menopause and makes women vulnerable to brittle bones. The male equivalent is testosterone, produced by the testes (balls to most of us).

Because oestrogen governs the way their bodies are formed, including their brains, hormones really do affect women's behaviour. Hence a woman's entitlement to blame them for:

- being assailed by lurid fantasies about the window cleaner
- purchasing tins of floor polish when the whole house is carpeted wall to wall
- snapping at her husband for mislaying her keys
- Bobbiting her partner for playing away while he is under the influence of testosterone.

Oestrogen is metabolised by the liver which might explain why women have a lower alcohol tolerance than men, especially when at their most fertile – their bodies are too busy making them fecund to process the booze. This may also be nature's crafty way of ensuring she is less inhibited at the very best time to conceive.

The Brain

Women's brains are also constructed differently. Men's brains are on average bigger by about 5 ounces – the weight of a small hamburger, without the bun.

Research reveals that women's brains contain a higher concentration of cells in the cortices associated with listening and language ability, have a bigger passageway connecting the left and right hemispheres of the brain and more movement of signals between the two hemispheres. This means that women:

- learn to talk earlier than men (there are signs that they start practising with their lips while still in the womb)

- display greater manual dexterity (female fingers are better at finicky jobs like computer assembly, sutures and applying nail-varnish)

- have more acute verbal skills ("Darling, your dinner is in the dog.")

- are less prone to dyslexia and stuttering

- pay more attention to detail. If a group of boys and girls are asked to draw a house, the boys will almost always draw the framework first, then add a chimney, whereas girls concentrate on the doors and windows (with curtains).

- chart a route by focusing on landmarks, rather than map or compass ("There was a bent lamppost on the corner"). Many men believe that women navigate conversations the same way.

In conversation you could show how these differences have been reinforced culturally over the aeons, and have become woven into the complex mix of genetic, social and evolutionary factors of which today's women are the product. In the past, when men went off in droves armed with weapons in search of bison, or any spare women they fancied, talk was superfluous. They could survive with grunts and hand signals. Meanwhile, the women were stuck in the cave with the babies – an environment which called for nurture, empathy and good communications:

"Nuts! I think we've used a bit too much digitalis."
"I've been at him for moons to fix that rock in the roof, but he's done nothing!"
"If you use these berries you can tenderise the aardvark."
"Talk about wildebeest dressed as calf, and she's overdone the woad again."
"Personally, I wouldn't touch him with a spear pole."
"That's the last time I'm telling you – don't draw on the walls."

GUILES AND GUISES

Whereas men go through various distinct phases in growing up (to use the term loosely) but end up as basically the same model, women encompass a bewildering variety of different types. They have a battery of disguises at their disposal, and select the ones that best suit them to achieve their own ends.

To complicate matters further, many of the guises overlap, and most women are capable of switching between even wildly incompatible ones to match the occasion. And since, to a woman, an occasion may be as brief as an argument-clinching sentence or a passing greeting, she can often seem to epitomise the full range simultaneously.

The system being therefore far from foolproof, you need not try to fathom it beyond recognising a few general traits.

Poor Little Me

Soft-spoken, prettily self-deprecating, and with a whim of iron, Poor Little Me has discovered early on that the helpless female usually gets everything done for her by indulgent parents and older siblings.

Seeing no reason to change a winning formula as she grows up, she makes great play of her physical feebleness, mechanical and intellectual incompetence and general dependence, and thus almost always gets her own way with minimum amount of trouble to herself.

This technique can be a great success with men, whose fragile egos are easily flattered, but it usually irritates or even infuriates other women. Knowing that women can always cope, they despise Poor Little

Me's pretence that she can't; they feel she is letting the side down by trading on the erroneous stereotype of the helpless female, and resent her easy entrapment of gullible would-be knights-errant. Above all, of course, they are jealous of her rate of success.

The downside is that Poor Little Me can become as clingy as she intended to be. Few men see through her because she dazzles them. Even other women find her hard to unmask.

It is impossible to win an argument with someone who says sweetly and simperingly: "I'm sure you're right, it's just that I have no memory/am so stupid about money/don't understand anything mechanical," and then goes serenely on to do exactly what she wanted to and what you swore you wouldn't countenance.

Bimbo

The oddest thing about Bimbos is that they really don't seem to mind the label. This could mean that they are as air-headed as the image they project, or that they have everything much better sussed than anyone gives them credit for. After all, it must be quite relaxing to sail through life turning heads, willing to be attentive to a series of egotistical males, and ready to party at the drop of a wallet.

On the surface, Bimbos have much in common with Poor Little Mes, but they lack the manipulativeness – all they want is a good time.

Most women, and about a quarter of men, deride them, but fairly indulgently: the general view tends to be that they really can't help it. Besides, the phenomenon is temporary. Bimbos mysteriously vanish in their mid-twenties, becoming trophy wives if they're lucky, or doormats if they aren't.

Bimbos are not subtle, and therefore their game is easily routed. Just stop paying.

Doormat

The Doormat subsumes all her own interests to the needs and demands of her family. Her husband, well aware that he should be contributing more to the housekeeping/parenting role than he does, but unwilling to forego the luxury of dinner on the table and his clothes picked up after him, tends to placate rather than help. Other women may talk bracingly to the Doormat about Open University courses, but will generally give up under a barrage of counter-arguments.

It is in nobody's interests for Doormats to change their ways. They are too useful as reliable cook/bottle-washers, emergency baby-sitters, errand runners and servicemen-letter-inners. So perhaps the best way to deal with them is to do what most people do, and use them shamelessly.

Earth Mother

The carer par excellence, she is programmed to understand and provide for everything anybody might need or want: she would embrace the whole human race if she could.

In childhood, Earth Mothers patiently mind younger siblings; at university they indulgently make coffee and toast at 3 a.m. for drunken fellow students searching for the meaning of life; in adulthood they nurture their own brood, any they may have inherited, those of their friends and neighbours, plus multifarious godchildren; at work they are the ones who answer plaintive phones on unattended desks.

They are admirable. But Earth Mothers unfortunately know what's good for everyone. As they cluck around their wholefood kitchen, breastfeeding the four year-old, they dispense endless homilies on how to sort out your own inadequate life. Ultimately they miss out, because people learn to avoid any area of conversation which might engender their voluminous advice.

Ballbreaker

Ballbreakers come in two distinct varieties: the ardent feminist to whom men are always, implacably, the enemy; and the intimidating career woman who manages to be feminine, sexy, and efficient at juggling work, family and leisure. Both kinds are just as alarming to women as they are to men.

You can disarm the feminist by agreeing earnestly with her on all points, and then go away and carry on in your own sweet way. You could try to undermine the super-achiever by quoting some of the statistics and opinions that have arisen in the course of the 1990s backlash against the concept of doing/having it all; but if she's really entrenched in her role, you will almost certainly fail. Better to express unqualified admiration for her, and admit the shortcomings that make you personally unable to compete.

Normal

This guise is the most cunning of them all. Women are never normal. Each and every one of them knows that she is utterly extraordinary and enigmatic.

SEX

Women need to feel a degree of sexual intimacy before sex becomes desirable. They need a sense of security and comfort, free from distraction, where they can relax and enjoy the totality of a deeply sensual experience – and probably black-out conditions to shield them from reality.

In a survey of women, nearly a third said that they could 'take or leave sex'; paradoxically, 83% of them believed that they derived as much pleasure from sex as men. But women bring to sex a rather different mind-set: they are more interested in how they are treated than in performance ratings. For women, intimacy sometimes results in sex; for men, sex sometimes results in intimacy.

It would be a mistake to infer from this that women do not have a corresponding sex drive. They do – especially when the oestrogen levels are right. Yet, whereas a man is bundled along by his testosterone-inflated sex drive, and may become physically uncomfortable if he goes more than a week without ejaculating, a woman can go for years without sex, applying a form of self-control of which most men are incapable. In Britain the average woman has 3.4 sexual partners over a lifetime – although nobody will admit to being the one who was only point four.

Virginity

This once-cherished notion has been largely suspended through lack of volunteers. Statistically it was on a hiding to nothing. If all men want to experiment before marrying a virgin, there is inevitably going to be a shortfall.

Men, if they give it a thought, believe that the hymen is a redoubtable membrane with the consistency of bubblegum. They may be confounded or relieved to discover that, because of energetic sports and use of tampons, many women barely have one to speak of. Women's experience of the 'first time' varies, and is less related to the resistance of the hymen than to the skill of their partners. Women divide into those who hardly noticed its breach, and those who would rather draw a veil over the whole event.

There is a tale of a young couple emerging from a quickie in the dark. The somewhat chastened man remarked that had he known the girl was a virgin, he would have gone about the matter more slowly. The girl retorted that had she understood his hurry, she would have removed her tights first.

Seduction

Traditionally, men make the first move. Or so they like to believe.

In fact, it is nearly always women who seduce men. They send out little signals with their eyes, they touch an arm, they remove an imaginary hair from a man's sleeve. Then comes a bit of feminine sleight of hand: they make a tactical retreat. It is not long before the average male comes charging down the hill with the whiff of the chase in his nostrils.

When men say they find a certain woman attractive, they often mean they think she is available, or at least that she is putting out availability signals (otherwise known as flirting). Men like to think they know how to read these signals, but unfortunately are probably not as good at doing so as other women – such as their wives.

A woman knows that there is no better way to cultivate a man's interest than to make him yearn for her – the time-honoured convention of 'playing hard to get'. This is done by adhering to some tried and tested rules, such as:

- delay answering his telephone messages
- never be free on the first date he suggests
- accept invitations from other men
- never agree to sex until he has demonstrated that he wants more than just your body.

Of course, any of these responses could also mean exactly what it seems to: that she simply isn't interested. Nevertheless, though most men dislike the idea of being played like a fish, they quite admire women for having a seduction plan. It's more than they have.

When women talk, they tend to look each other in the eye. Men generally avoid eye-contact when talking to other men, thus doing away with the primitive need to lock horns and establish who is dominant. So if women are not interested, all they have to do is look away. The sign goes up: no vacancies.

Orgasms

Remember when you watch the urgent clash of flesh, and gasps of mutual ecstasy in steamy Hollywood bonkbusters, that the average cinema-goer has an attention span of about 45 seconds. Even Sharon Stone confesses that she did women a disservice in *Basic Instinct* by suggesting that they could reach orgasm in about 30 seconds flat. This is just not how the female body works, and anyone who suggests otherwise is either a good actress, deluded or blessed by the gods.

17

For women, orgasm is not necessarily the goal. Physical intimacy, closeness, emotional bonding may give perfectly satisfactory sex. This is fortunate given that, according to the *Hite Report*, three-quarters of men ejaculate within two minutes of penetration. It is statements of this kind which lead women to believe that: 'There is no such thing as a frigid woman; there is only an inadequate man.'

The male obsession with orgasm leads 50% of women to fake it in order to reassure their partner that he is not a failure – and nobody who has ever seen *When Harry Met Sally* can be in any doubt that women are supreme bluffers in this respect. Surveys also indicate that about the same number never reach a climax through intercourse. And 10% have never had one at all.

The problem is often that, for men, foreplay is a curtain-raiser whereas, for women, touching and stroking are a crucial part of the act (Acts I-V, if not the grand finale).

Men are charged with several million long-tailed gametes that are eager to get on with their job just as soon as optimum position for dispatch is achieved. This may be due to an instinctive fear. In the savannahs of Africa, he might have been jumped on by a sabre-toothed tiger if he lingered too long. Unfortunately, it seems that the male body has not evolved in five million years to take account of the modern fashion for lingering – unless it's for sleep.

An added anxiety for women is the concept of the multiple orgasm. Men, with their competitive instincts in the Sexual Olympics, often feel the need to prove themselves good lovers by hammering away to try and achieve this, and many women feel that because the event is documented as achievable, they are failures if they don't achieve it themselves – even if their single orgasms rival Krakatoa.

Most women conclude at some point in their lives that the female body is badly designed. The clitoris, the main source of female orgasm, is a long way from centre stage; practically in the upper circle. Not the choicest place to guarantee stimulation during intercourse, especially in the man-on-top missionary position (which is probably why the killjoy missionaries recommended it). As with a dance tune, too often women only just begin to get the riff when the rhythm is over.

Men are frequently unaware that, though the source of women's pleasure may be the size of a peanut, it is armed with all the sensitivity of a six-inch penis. The degree of delicacy in approaching such a minute hand-grenade can take years to get right. Until that time arrives, many women would rather read a good book.

Contraception

In a survey, women were asked to cite the three most significant factors affecting female emancipation. They gave:

- the Pill
- the right to vote
- the washing machine.

Contraception liberates women to pursue the physical side of sex without feeling that they have to tie it to emotional commitment, though this does not mean that they will not also be on the lookout for that special person to whom they can make a long-term commitment. In other words, they can pursue sex in the way men have always done.

You can, of course, suggest that men have shown themselves willing to bear a greater responsibility for contraception, but be careful of mentioning the concept of the male pill. This is something of a dead end. The male pill has been shown to be effective, but even if women could trust men to take it, the progesterone (female hormone) content reduces the male sex-drive, which rather defeats the object.

Promiscuity

If a man sleeps around he is considered a bit of a lad. If a woman sleeps around she is considered a tramp. Even women think so, although they may use a gentler term such as 'slut'.

This disparity goes back to the primitive need of men (even male gorillas) to be sure that the offspring that they raise is their own and not someone else's. A society dominated by males produces a patrilineal system of inheritance, making it even more vital that the father knows that his heirs are really his. Social mores were formed around such patterns, and women were probably too exhausted to argue.

In any case this attitude does not take account of the philanthropic service performed by promiscuous women in meeting the excessive need of men. There is a phenomenon in the animal world – among apes and elephants, for instance – known as the 'sneaky rutter'. When the dominant male (read husband) is distracted, a weaker rival male has a quick and surreptitious fling with one of his females (read wife), who is usually a willing party. It might be inferred from this that animals have an instinctive urge to broaden the genetic pool. Women who put themselves around could really have the good of the human race at heart.

FEELINGS

Motherhood

There is a mystique about motherhood which seems to assume that just because women can do it, all of them should want to.

Pregnancy can mean morning sickness, varicose veins, the physical shrinking of the brain, not to mention a craving for pickled onions and pawpaw. Any other condition that caused such symptoms would be under trial for a cure. It is no surprise that a fair number of women are not that keen.

Many women consider their role in reproduction to be nature's final act of vengeance against them – or even as definitive proof that God is a man. Why else, after the traumas of childbirth, would they gaze misty-eyed at a squalling bundle of dependency, and immediately, of their own free will, resolve to repeat the whole grisly experience?

It is a good thing that women are programmed to love their babies. Any other activity that caused sleepless nights and loss of free time would be avoided at all costs.

The urge to be a mother, if it visits at all, can hit the single woman just as powerfully as the one who believes that she has found her life partner, and nowadays she can gratify it with the help of an anonymous donor. Scientists are apparently near to perfecting an artificial womb, which could help make the process less harrowing. Once that has been achieved, women could decide to eschew the physical process entirely by putting on a Brave New World-type production. A few choice male players might be kept, like prize bulls, in order to maintain supplies for the sperm bank.

However, women are not about to grab fertility and run. Men are still required, and their services are appreciated. But there has been a radical shift in the ball park, so to speak.

In any case, to hand childbirth over to a laboratory would be to hand over the trump card. And nothing will ever usurp the strange unfathomable sentiment that a woman can feel when she meets a man to whom she is instantly attracted and thinks: "I want to have his children."

When making their choice, women would be doing themselves a favour if they heeded the advice of one mother: "Marry a man with a small head."

Guilt

Women feel guilty about everything, all the time. They feel guilty about their weight, their appearance, their careers, their mothering skills, the whiteness of their washes – even about dying. "I don't mind dying, but it's leaving my man," fretted Rose Rodin, the sculptor's wife. "Who will look after him? What will happen to the poor thing?"

Above all, women feel guilty about not being perfect. They read articles in glossy magazines about 'having it all', padded with examples of Superwomen who effortlessly juggle high-flying careers, idyllic family lives, culinary triumphs, fashion-model figures and superb taste (with the help of a lot of money and an army of paid aid), and are racked with self-reproach for not managing it themselves (with the help of nobody).

Then they read articles about the folly of sacrificing quality of life and peace of mind to Superwoman ideals, and feel conscience-stricken about that too.

Luckily, women are ever-adaptable as well as ever-guilty. As Golda Meir robustly said when accused of neglecting her children (she was busy founding Israel at the time): "You can get used to anything if you have to, even to feeling perpetually guilty."

You cannot bluff a woman out of feeling guilty by either:

1. Encouragingly citing her strengths (it will only make her believe that anything you don't mention as a strength is a weakness).

2. Telling her she mustn't feel guilty (she will instantly assume she has something she hadn't even thought of yet to feel guilty about).

Saying Sorry

Men hate saying 'Sorry'. To them it is an admission of failure – or at least that they have been found out. But as well as using the word to apologise, women also say 'Sorry' to express general sympathy and regret. Men's inability to grasp this distinction means that, when a woman says she is sorry about his tale of woe, he feels she has exonerated him from all blame.

A Good Cry

Although it is nowadays officially acceptable – even desirable – for men to cry, they will never be a match for women. Conditioned to stifle their emotions from birth, men will never understand how women can, in the right circumstances, claim to enjoy 'a good cry'.

It has been suggested that women may like a good

cry at a weepie film because it gives them the catharsis of tears without the real emotional pain of their own lives. In other situations, tears are the physical release of pent-up emotions – not necessarily misery. Rage can precipitate women to tears more often than is generally imagined, and so can being happy.

Tears make men very uncomfortable, because they feel something is expected of them, but don't know what. Even women dither between tentative pats and strangled noises of sympathy or a crushing bear-hug.

Rest assured, often no action is required; the tears are actually the solution.

Friendship

Friendship is enormously important to women – more important, indeed, than sex. It is also quite different for women than it is for men. Men want friends to play with (for example as golf partners, or as people with whom to go to the pub, watch the Cup Final and strip engines), whereas women want friends to talk to. Women have friends the way men have hobbies.

Ever since their far-off hunter-gathering days, the female instinct to socialise has remained so strong that it may well be regarded as the driving force behind human social behaviour. It is said that women are more interested in people, and men more interested in things – which goes some way towards explaining why men are rather better at mending cars than at small talk.

Women develop very close friendships with other women, often operating on intuitive understanding, as kindred spirits. Part of it is about using each other as sounding boards, sharing personal feelings, and being a psychiatric support group.

A woman's female friends are also her network, her information service and her chief source of cultural and intellectual debate.

It is a curious phenomenon, therefore, that women are prepared to reorientate their social lives entirely towards a male partner in a manner that is not paralleled by men and their male pals. When a woman marries, and even more so when she starts to raise a family, her social horizons change and her old chums are dropped in favour of new ones with similar concerns – and burdens.

Women would really like to be friends with men, but they can't get round the fact that most men won't indulge in free-range conversation – and to a woman, that's what friendship is all about. When they find a man who will chat about anything from communism to carpet shampoo, they stick to him like clingfilm because he is that rare creature who is able to dissociate himself from gender and talk about ideas.

Women want to fall in love with a man's mind – which isn't easy but explains why many form close friendships with homosexual men, who have the knack of being interested in the same things as women without involving a whole lot of psycho-sexual baggage as well.

You could postulate that the most fulfilling thing a woman can do is to feel really connected to another human being – whereas the most fulfilling thing a man can do is reach a climax. Sad, really.

ATTITUDES

To Men

'A woman need know but one man well in order to understand all men; whereas a man may know all women and understand not one of them,' wrote American journalist Helen Rowland in the 1920s.

It doesn't seem to bother men that women persistently make rude remarks about them, possibly because they are so used to it that they no longer really feel the barbs, or because they are so conceited they think women are joking. This is lucky, since women find very little to say in men's favour, and such plus points as they are prepared to concede tend to be grudging ("They're quite handy to have around") or downright condescending:

> Women's faults are many,
> Men have only two:
> Everything they say,
> And everything they do.

Women constantly look for the good qualities of men: a sense of fair play, consideration for others, respect, a genuinely caring attitude, modesty, old-fashioned courtesy, and a sense of independence and individuality which is on the manageable side of psychotic. They seldom do find them, however, and if they do, they cherish them like endangered species – which makes it easy for women gathered together and swapping anecdotes to end up feeling decidedly superior.

Convinced of their own complexity, women just can't believe it possible that men are as transparent as they seem; that what you see is more or less all you get. "The trouble with some women," said Cher Bono, "is they get all excited about nothing – and then marry him." Women are convinced that somewhere in men must lurk a hidden store of untapped thoughts, insights and emotions, an inner self similar to their own, and that they only need find the key to unlock it. If a woman can find a way to a man's inner self she feels that precious sense of being the only one who knows him. She might be the only one who wants to.

Women find this search for the non-existent lode in men both frustrating and tantalising: men owe much of women's fascination with them to the false hope of its existence. This may be the most successful bluff on women they have ever achieved.

Yet whatever they may say, in practice women are remarkably tolerant of men. They are prepared to like them despite their failings; patiently bolster male egos knowing full well that men won't reciprocate; give them the benefit of the doubt far beyond the point when doubt is a reasonable hypothesis.

But whether they tolerate them, like them or love them, women find men a constant disappointment. Even their own sons, apples of their eye, end up abandoning them for another woman.

The Drop Knickers Effect

There is a paucity of men whom women find irresistibly attractive, upon whom to unleash their passion. Men are notorious for being indiscriminate. Women are far more picky.

Men might take comfort from the fact that it is virtually impossible to predict which men will be judged by women to be attractive and which will be given the thumbs-down. Advertising companies play safe by veering between meticulous males with all-round appeal, and designer-stubbled scruffs, looking studiedly debauched.

A survey conducted by a television game show found out what a woman first noticed in a man. Top of the list, in order, were: eyes, bottom, clothes, cash, teeth, hair. Eyes, of course, are an important key to character. Bottoms are a feminine indulgence. Women find something very appealing about the shape of lean male buttocks, especially when tightly wrapped in a pair of jeans, and are fascinated by the way men have dents where women have bulges. It would, however, be a very foolish male bluffer who relied on this attribute alone for his appeal.

Revealing all is not guaranteed to produce the ultimate sensation: on balance, more likely the opposite. As a female stripper teases her g-string, the males watch goggle-eyed, their salivating silence broken only by heavy breathing. Women watching a male stripper cheer and heckle raucously; they shriek with laughter. A gleaming, muscular male body is quite a treat, and sexy to boot, but it is also hugely funny. The question is, will he go all the way and produce the funniest thing of all?

The naked truth is that women are more likely to be attracted to a man when he has his clothes on.

Ask any woman which male film stars make her go weak at the knees; which ones would make her throw husband, reputation and knickers to the wind, and the answer is extremely few: Donald Sutherland, Jean-Paul Belmondo (the *joli-laid* look), Sean Connery (worth mentioning in the company of bald men), Kirk Douglas (that dimple), Clint Eastward (if wearing a poncho), Denzel Washington (leather trousers in *Much Ado About Nothing*), Brad Pitt, George Clooney (bedroom eyes), Cary Grant, Clark Gable (they don't have to be alive).

Harrison Ford does well – particularly that scene in the garage in *Witness* when he and the Amish woman look at each other, burning with illicit desire. Note that he does not have to remove a stitch of clothing to achieve this.

Men may well become disheartened as the list of rejected Hollywood icons gets longer and longer, written off because they do not look trustworthy, fancy themselves too much, are too hairy, have no apparent intelligence, or lack strength of character. What hope is left for lesser mortals?

Given the statistical chances of winning the man of their dreams, women usually have to make do with second best – which is where certain qualities come into play, such as good company, kindness, and clean fingernails.

But the one quality which is guaranteed to win a woman's heart is a sense of humour. Lack of humour will often be cited as the Achilles heel of an otherwise desirable man.

Above all, women like men who show an interest in them. They can be as ugly as sin, but if they make a woman feel important and cherished, if they can amuse and entertain, the world is their oyster. The 18th-century reformer John Wilkes was notoriously ugly, yet remarkably successful with women. "I need half an hour to talk away my face," he explained.

In fact, it is a common occurrence for attractive women to chose ugly men: they can be relied on not to stray. This is possibly an instinctive throw-back to the days when it was important to keep a man close to base when the babies started arriving, and it appears to have some correlation in hormonal responses. Austrian researchers have studied the effect of body odour on stimulating attraction. Using T-shirts impregnated with scent associated with attractive and less attractive men, they gave these to women to sniff throughout their menstrual cycle. They concluded that women seemed more attracted to the scent associated with the better looking men when at the beginning and end of the cycle – but in the middle, when they were at their most fertile, they were more attracted to the uglier ones.

To Relationships

When men see an attractive woman, they fantasise about sex. When women see an attractive man, they fantasise about a relationship – charming, agreeable company over dinner, friendship and comfort. Sex does not necessarily come into it. What really matters is two spirits enmeshed and invigorated by a magical coalescence: this could be for ever. Most men are blissfully unaware of this difference in attitude, or refuse to believe it.

It is a mystery to women why men should be afraid of commitment to a relationship, when long-term relationships so patently benefit men more than women. It is a known fact that divorced men die younger if they do not remarry.

Thanks to millennia of biological programming and their empathetic, social nature, most women want relationships, and are less afraid of committing to them than men – or, indeed, than is wise. They will settle for a good deal less than their fantasies: the occasional compliment, gift of flowers, dinner out or meal cooked for them, perhaps even a conversation, is enough to persuade a woman that she has found a truly caring man.

To Other Women

The biggest confidence trick ever played on women is the idea that other women are on their side. They aren't. Men may be the traditional enemy, but other women are the fifth column. Other women – unless they are family or friends, and sometimes not even then – are their rivals.

When a woman walks into a room at a business meeting or a party, another woman watching her may automatically think to herself, "Is she prettier than me? Younger, better dressed?"

It would be bad enough to appear unpresentable to a man, far worse before a group of women. Women have a knack of undermining each other and can do so with great precision. They insinuate cricitism through apparent compliments, such as:

- "You're looking very pretty tonight." (You're usually so plain.)
- "She was just letting her hair down." (She was making a complete fool of herself.)
- "I always think that dress suits you so well." (Are you still wearing that old thing?)
- "She always takes such trouble with her make-up." (She needs to.)

To Daughters

Daughters are a threat to their mothers from the day they are born. Loved, indeed adored, at one level, they innocently arouse jealousy, irritation, envy, resentment and fury on another. Men do not understand the hostility which a mother can feel for her daughter just because the younger of the two has borrowed a 36D cup bra.

A wife might suggest to her husband that Wednesday would be a good night to go and see a new film but will be told he has too much work to do, his team is playing a championship match, or that he cannot stand romantic comedies. Her daughter will then come along suggesting exactly the same thing and he will agree without hesitation. She can wind her father around her little finger.

A mother may buy herself a sweater in a particular shade of blue and show it proudly to her daughter, only to be told that the colour is 'awful'. Twenty-four hours later the sweater will go missing, only to be found on the daughter when she returns from a party. "It was cold," she will explain, "and anyway it suits me better than you."

Daughters, especially teenage daughters, are programmed to annoy their mothers beyond belief. It is a knack acquired early on that results in family scenes which always end in tears, recriminations, hugs and kisses and the mother giving her daughter whatever garment was stolen from her because she feels guilty for having been so mean. What seems to be forgotten during these episodes is that, once upon a time, the mother herself was a daughter.

To Marriage

'Bigamy is having one husband too many,' wrote Erica Jong, 'Monogamy is the same.' Men get a wife out of marriage: women get more work.

Nevertheless, getting married as opposed to being married – which is when women discover that 'happy ever after' is not quite the truth – remains an ideal objective for many women (or at least for their mothers). Having a Mateus Rosé wedding is the height of delight

– floating across the meadow, in a white organza dress and dainty satin slippers, the groom moving towards her, his arms outstretched – this is the stuff of dreams.

Despite the harsh fact that in Britain one in three marriages now ends in divorce (one in two in the US), people spend more on formal white weddings than ever before. Perhaps the solemn, public commitment acts as a talisman against divorce, and the expense of the big day gives warning of how much more costly the decree nisi might be.

'It is a woman's business to get married as soon as possible,' mused George Bernard Shaw, 'and a man's to keep unmarried as long as he can.' Many women still feel that they haven't achieved their full potential unless they've netted a mate.

Their conditioning requires a male partner whom they will have to coax, cajole and manipulate into acting in anything approximate to his ideal role. The trouble is that men soon learn that their spouses are expert at adapting, especially in relation to themselves. They know that there is:

- The woman who can do it and does it.
- The woman who can do it, but waits to find a man to do it for her.
- The woman who says "Darling, can you do it?" and knows she's going to have to do it in the end.
- The woman who has long since given up and doesn't even ask. She just does it.

In reality, what women need in marriage is a wife.

PRACTICALITIES

Coping

Women have a special aptitude for multi-tasking – i.e. managing several jobs or ideas at the same time. Men perform better at complicated linear problems, such as working out the trajectory of the football to the goal, but they usually cannot concentrate on anything else until they've done it. It takes a woman to load the washing machine while minding the baby, hearing the 5-year-old's spellings, cooking dinner, planning tomorrow's wardrobe, creating a snappy slogan for her next multinational marketing campaign, and deciding how to get her husband to ring his mother.

One of the key points about understanding women is the realisation that it isn't just that women can juggle several tasks at once – they are actually congenitally incapable of thinking of fewer than three things at a time. This is why so many female characters created by men seem implausibly two-dimensional. It may also be why 400 times more men than women commit suicide: the women are worrying that if they step off the world, the mince they left in the fridge will go off before it is eaten.

It is certainly why men are so often baffled by women's conversational leaps, and so blithely certain that whatever havoc men may cause, women will 'cope'. Women also secretly know they will cope, and even pride themselves on it. Coping is what women do.

Women at Work

More women than ever before are in paid employment, and in many ways the world of work has given in gracefully: maternity leave schemes, sexual harassment codes, flexi-time and crèches are now either statutory or are at least becoming widespread. Yet on average women still earn less than men for the same job, get fewer perks, and often hit an invisible yet tangible 'glass ceiling' halfway up the promotional ladder – only 11% of managers are women. Men find it hard to believe this barrier exists: "I just don't see it," they say, citing equal opportunities legislation. They wouldn't – it's glass.

For some time it was assumed that women, in order to succeed, had to behave like men – hiring and firing, confronting opposition head on and carving up rivals. These days the work culture is changing with the recognition that women's special aptitudes can bring identifiable business benefits. Women make work easier because they:

- are better at communicating
- are good at teamwork
- do umpteen things at once
- compromise without feeling any loss of face
- will make the coffee or take the minutes, provided it is made categorically clear that it isn't in their job description
- keep the grapevine going, along with the potted plants.

Yet statistics indicate that women still have to be considerably better than men to get the job offer. They can take comfort from the fact that, as Charlotte Whitton said when she was Mayor of Ottawa, "Whatever women do, they must do twice as well as men to be thought half as good. Luckily, this is not difficult."

Maybe it is because they know this that most women prefer to work for a man than for another woman – men are easier to manipulate than women who have achieved success, know how tough it is, and are correspondingly hard on their underlings.

In spite of their inferior promotion prospects and remuneration, it has been found that women actually do more than men in the same job. All those things that fall into nobody's job description, such as putting more paper in the photocopier, checking there will be enough folders for the sales conference and explaining company policies to juniors, are done by women. A man may spend hours (of business time) writing memos about them, but it wouldn't occur to him to deal with them himself.

This could be because women are not as status-ridden, but to some men it can seem intimidating. By crossing demarcation lines as invisible to women as the glass ceiling is to men, women threaten the delicate, complex structure of power in men's highly politicised office world. As G. K. Chesterton said: "If you convey to a woman that something ought to be done, there is always a dreadful danger that she will suddenly do it."

Beware of citing examples of much-publicised female high-flyers: you are likely to get the retort that these are only newsworthy because they are still perceived as unusual. And when they fall, the press go into a kind of feeding frenzy, savage enough to leave male rivals feeling quite left out. Women in politics are singled out for particularly thorough scrutiny. Should they turn out to have a voice of their own, to give as good as they get in the combative atmosphere of Parliament, they are quickly labelled brusque, sharp-tongued, a termagant. It takes a male MP years of haranguing and carping to achieve this kind of reputation.

What it is then that keeps women trying to batter down the doors to the last few uncongenial bastions of male domination – sewerage maintenance, army boot camps, Mount Athos? Probably the same compulsion that makes small children put beans in their ears: the fact that they have been warned off lends allure. Besides, some male bastions have proved worth besieging in the past. And women have an irresistible urge to try them all out for size.

Housework

These days, men can and do cook, iron and vacuum, and have even been known to clean the bath. But surveys show that women still spend four to five times as long on domestic chores as their helpful husbands.

Men tend to see housework as an option, a special extra job they do to demonstrate how modern they are: they are genuinely baffled by the fury it can rouse in a woman if they innocently ask "Can I help?" Wives don't want husbands to help: they want them to recognise that they bear equal responsibility for running the household.

The fact is that men can tolerate a greater degree of grime and disorder than women before they even notice it – so it is usually the woman who heads for the broom cupboard first. Happily, this does at least pay off in property values: when a couple sells their separate flats to buy a house together, in 90% of cases the woman's sells first.

Map Reading

Because many women will turn maps upside down so the roads drawn match their direction of travel, they are often assumed to be lousy map-readers. Yet in other circumstances, such as peeking at memos across desks, reading upside down is regarded as clever.

Some women are lousy map-readers, as are some men. But being curious, women also want to be watching what is going on outside the windows instead of staring fixedly at the atlas on their knees, which everyone knows makes you carsick.

Many women have overcome their disadvantages and become perfectly competent navigators. They are frequently hampered, however, by male drivers who refuse to believe they really do mean 'Turn left', ignore the instruction, or argue that straight on must be quicker.

Punctuality

When a woman arrives at a rendezvous with a man three minutes after the appointed time, she is late. When a man breezes in at nine for the dinner that was ready at 7.30, having stopped off for a quick one or seven on the way home, he was unavoidably detained.

There are people of both genders who are congenitally poor timekeepers, but, these menaces aside, women are in fact rarely unpunctual. And if they are, they didn't mean to be.

There is a fundamental misunderstanding between the sexes over what punctuality is. Men, with their more linear thought processes, and a certain degree of selfishness, want to get on with the next item on their agenda as soon as they reach it. Women, being more flexible in their approach and needing to incorporate all sorts of diversions en route – dropping off the dry cleaning, picking up the children, returning the library books, looking for a phone box, waiting for the wheel clamp removers – find that time just doesn't stretch the way it should.

Many women also deliberately arrive ten minutes after the time agreed, to avoid the risk of waiting alone in a wine bar, restaurant or, worse, on a street corner because of ......men.

FOIBLES

Intuition

Women take great pride in their intuition. They find it hard to accept that men are not armed with the same sense of instinctive insight – and are consistently let down by this. It is the basis of one of the key areas of misunderstanding between the sexes.

Men usually fail to notice if anyone has a problem until it is either brought to their notice or has become too obvious to ignore. They then presume that resolution lies in immediately proposing solutions. Men like to appear decisive. Women tend to pre-empt acutely problematic situations, thanks to their well-developed antennae.

'A woman's guess is much more accurate than a man's certainty,' wrote Rudyard Kipling; and even sour William Hazlitt grudgingly acknowledged that 'Women never reason, and therefore they are (comparatively) seldom wrong.'

Women listen more intently, and are capable of picking up other people's moods and feelings by reading infinitesimal signs on their faces, in their eyes, or in their movements. They can sense in an instant if something is not right – a flash of a glance or a hesitancy which conceals an untruth.

Much of women's intuition can be explained by the mental and social ways they operate. Women are genuinely interested in people, and spend a lot of time working out what makes them tick. Thus what may seem like a snap character assessment may well be based on reasoning, proceeding from particular cases to general conclusions, which is a scientifically respectable principle of analysis. They will diagnose someone's lifestyle from the contents of their supermarket trolley: several children, a difficult teenage vegetarian, three dogs, overweight husband with irregular motions and a potting shed.

Many men profess to be completely baffled by the way women can leap from speculation to certainty without due process of deduction between the two. Women are largely indulgent of this male bafflement, partly because it's no more than they expect, and partly because it gives them the upper hand.

Gossip

Gossip is an essential component of women's friendships, and not at all the character assassination men often seem to think it is. As American broadcaster Barbara Walters said: "Show me someone who never gossips, and I'll show you someone who isn't interested in people."

Ask a woman for a description of a person and you will get the full identikit from height and figure to good teeth and plucked eyebrows. Ask a man and you will probably get "I didn't really notice. I only saw her legs." In their quest to understand everything about everybody, women analyse themselves, each other, and the possible motives behind the slightest deed or word in obsessive detail.

"But what were you talking about?" a bemused man may ask a woman who has just spent two hours on the phone to someone she saw only that morning, or is just setting off to meet. In general, men regard conversation strictly as a means of imparting essential information; they don't understand that to women, all information is essential, and gossip is therefore the vital currency of life.

Going to the Lavatory in Pairs

If men got up in pairs to go to the lavatory, their relationship would immediately come under question. Yet women do it all the time, and nobody reads anything into it. Nor is it simply that the one who said "I'll come with you" had been crossing her legs for hours, but was too shy to mention her need in mixed company.

There are a number of explanations for this tribal rite:

- Women seek safety in numbers.
- They want to get together to exchange confidences.
- They don't trust the other woman enough to leave her alone with the men, so they encourage her to come too.
- They don't want to use the lavatory at all, just the mirror to check their make-up.

Basically, nobody really understands women's reasons for communal comfort stops. It could be an extension of the female propensity to match each other's hormonal rhythms, or simply that they are just naturally sociable. As the Irish say, "Will you walk with me to take the naked look off me?"

Feminine Wiles

Little girls charm their fathers into a suspension of rational thought. Teenage girls plot every move they make. Married women give their husbands as much rope as they think is necessary for them to swing back to their way of thinking. But women deny that they operate anything as nebulous and sinister as a 'wile'. These are legitimate tactics.

Revenge

Beware the woman scorned. Every now and then she reaches the front page of the national press, for carving up her ex-husband's entire wardrobe, for throwing bleach over his Lamborghini, or for attempting to ensure no other woman will enjoy the pleasure of his most intimate assets.

It's a question of emotional investment. If a man has been scorned, he would rather pretend it hasn't happened. A scorned woman is engulfed by loss: she may have given the best years of her life to that man, her youthful looks, her fertility. She has learnt to know him better than he knows himself, and made untold compromises to accommodate him. She could forgive him everything he did while he was still with her, but nothing once he has gone. Above all, she cannot forgive him for no longer finding her desirable.

It is painful enough to face the fact that he has exchanged her for a younger model – but even more distressing that he is treated with understanding, sympathy, even admiration by everyone else. Being abandoned is a desperately lonely business. Few seem willing to join the scorned woman in building the pyre and hammering in the stake to which her ex deserves to be lashed.

So it is no surprise that she feels vengeful, and expresses this with her own brand of urban guerilla tactics – connecting the telephone to a talking timetable in Brazil, dampening a carpet and sowing it with cress seeds, hiding fish heads behind the dashboard. She may feel that TV's Roseanne Barr had it just about right when she said: "I'm not upset at getting divorced, but I'd rather be a widow."

Nagging

It is important to understand that a woman does not nag, she reminds. This point cannot be made too often. It is a fact that should be underlined several times over, at regular intervals throughout the day, and pinned to the kitchen noticeboard. Women do not nag.

Even if you may be under the impression that a woman is nagging, going on and on about something, she is not actually nagging, but reminding, and it is probably for your own good. There is absolutely no point in reading any further until you have taken this idea on board.

Nagging is not a female characteristic; this is a misapprehension put about by hen-pecked husbands who should know better. They are simply being apprised of the fact that they have not done what they said they were going to do, and need to be prompted, regularly, otherwise it won't get done.

Besides, once men realise that they can rely on women to remind them of the simple things that would otherwise clutter their minds, they come to depend on it. So they need to be reminded. Regularly.

Cattiness

Women believe they can get away with the sort of remarks that get men shot down in flames. Being catty is deemed a noble pursuit, like duelling. At its best its rapier precision can win the admiration, respect and terror of both sexes. "Boy George is all Britain needs," declared Joan Rivers. "Another queen who can't dress."

Their excuse for this behaviour is that for centuries they were physically, legally and socially dependent on men whom they had to flatter and beguile at every turn for fear of being abandoned, so they had no other means to assert themselves besides denigrating men, or other women who might usurp them. In fact, like cats, they just have this savage streak which they are quite unable to control.

But generally cattiness is more about mockery and teasing than aggression. Women tend to look wryly at life from the underside – it's the view they're most used to. Dorothy Parker was an expert practitioner: when told that rival journalist Clare Booth Luce was invariably kind to her inferiors she asked; "And where does she find them?"

The truly deft catty remark can often contain a nugget of universal truth: "The trouble with Jane is that she's still young enough to think that one man may be better than another."

Shopping

Though many women actually hate shopping, the fact remains that by and large women shop in a way few men do. It certainly isn't about acquiring material possessions: a dedicated female shopper can come back as happy from an all-day expedition with no purchases as with a lorryload. On the other hand, just buying a lipstick can give her a kick.

Shopping can stimulate endorphins (the body's own morphia) which temporarily promotes a feel-good factor and, like chocolate, it can quickly become addictive.

Appearance

The first thing a woman thinks of when asked to go somewhere is "What am I going to wear?"

In a truly egalitarian society women would take as much trouble to dress as many men. That is to say, they would frequently sport dirty hair, and recycle crumpled clothes from the laundry basket when they ran out of clean ones.

Or perhaps not. Presentation is important to women. Their clothes serve as a pick-me-up on down days or as a suit of armour, from inside which they can confidently outface a hostile world. However, deciding upon the right outfit – the one that brings a glint of approval or, even better, a gleam of envy to another woman's eyes – is a cause for anxiety. How to find the outfit that proclaims the wearer to be simultaneously fashionable, at ease with her body and successfully in control of her life?

Take for example a casual lunch party where the hostess insists that you must 'come as you are'. The men will take this literally, and make an uninterrupted journey from under the car to the hostess's door in oil-smeared jeans and a holey jersey with dead leaves still stuck to it. "Leave me alone," he will insist when his wife tries to dust him off as they walk up the garden path. "She said 'come as you are', didn't she?"

His wife will have her own very different interpretation of this dress code which will represent, minimally, the third set of clothes she tried on that morning.

Men would be wise not to question this. Women love dressing up; they love to have an occasion to put on their glad rags, especially if the occasion demands a hat. But, more and more, they have come to realise the benefits of dressing like a man; discovered the liberation that proceeds, not only from the bliss of covering defects under dateless trousers and jacket, but also from eliminating the time and stress usually involved with choice.

The more women assume an outwardly take-me-seriously, unfussy style of clothing, the happier they are to indulge in frivolities underneath. As they did not wear knickers at all until the Victorian era, they could be making up for lost time. However, being given bright red silk lingerie for Valentine's Day might invite the question: "Is this your present, or mine?"

Pretty Woman

To men, and to most women as well, it must seem that life's a breeze for a pretty woman. Doors open for her that remain firmly closed for the rest of the world; when she walks into a room, sullen men start to sparkle, rich potential husbands jump out of the woodwork, the whole world seems brighter and sexier and more like a spread from *Hello!* magazine. She is even able to earn 10% more than plainer female counterparts.

In fact, good looks can be a terrible blight. Most men will not be able to talk to pretty women without having 'fwaw! she's gorgeous!' written all over their faces. Most women will look at them with steely eyes.

Another difficulty arises: men appear to find it hard to believe that a woman can be both beautiful and intelligent – 'not just a pretty face'. They can become so taken with the gift-wrapping that it doesn't occur to them there might be real gifts inside. Thus in business, prettiness can be as much a disadvantage to an intelligent woman as ugliness can be to anyone else.

Then there is the question of ageing: a pretty woman may define herself by her looks, so what is left when it fades?

But some pretty women manage to sail through in triumph, skilled and intelligent enough to be grateful for nature's gifts and know how to handle the pitfalls. And all young girls still want to grow up to be pretty.

Dieting

Very few women conform to the perceived ideal for the female shape, and virtually all of them worry about it. Surveys are disturbing. For instance, it has been found that in job interviews women with a low 'hip-to-waist' ratio are more likely to succeed. In other words they look more male. The editor of *Yes!* (a magazine for larger women) puts it brutally: 'It isn't true and it isn't fair, but ultimately curvaceous women are seen as stupid, lazy and greedy.'

One counter-argument lies in two other surveys revealing that women with narrower hips also have higher testosterone levels – and so do violent female offenders.

No constructive comments will stop a woman who is discontented with her body shape from dieting. Over 50% of Western women are on a diet at any one time. Women diet despite the well-publicised fact that dieting doesn't work. They do not do so simply to achieve the optimum weight for their figure and health. They diet because they secretly hope (even though they know it isn't true) that eating a lunchtime rusk which tastes about as good as its box will turn a Dolly Parton shape into a Kate Moss one. And that this will make them happy.

You could make derogatory remarks about 'the body fascists' – the fashion, advertising and self-styled health industry – or you could talk dreamily of other eras. The Venus de Milo is a BIG woman. Marilyn Monroe was decidedly voluptuous by today's standards.

Historically, the perception of the female form relates to child-bearing. When big families were desirable, so were heavy-breasted women with hips broad enough to drop a string of babies without obstetrical techniques not yet invented. All this changed in the 1920s with the flat-chested, bobbed-hair, beanpole look of the flappers when women first got a real taste of – and for – independence: it went briefly into abeyance in the 1950s with the need to repopulate after World War II, reappeared with the 1960s Sexual Revolution (the Pill was introduced in 1960) and has remained ever since. In the modern woman's mind 'thin' means 'youth' – the androgynous teenager.

As soon as a female pop icon or film star puts on excess pounds, some female journalist tears her to shreds. The following week, the same journalist will bewail the fashion which drives schoolgirls to anorexia. (Nine out of ten cases of anorexia and bulimia are women.) It is a woman who will describe a plump, dishevelled, but visibly happy mother of two as having 'let herself go'. Yet leading retailers confirm that women have been the same size for years. It is the ideal which is shrinking.

TOUCHY SUBJECTS

Intelligence

'A woman who has the misfortune of knowing anything,' wrote the 19th-century novelist Frances Trollope, 'should conceal it as well as she can.'

It is a sad truth that while men can stomach sparkles of intelligence from a woman, they find too much intellect indigestible. Intelligent women are a threat, and women have to take this into account if they wish to make headway with men. Men need to feel they are superior in the brainpower department. Women have to waste considerable amounts of their ingenuity and wit pretending that this is the case. It was a man who ruefully admitted: "Women are more intelligent than men. They have to be, to convince us so often that the opposite is true."

As an added complication, most women genuinely want their partner to be their intellectual superior: in any random survey, they will identify the man as the more intelligent of the partnership (as, of course, will the men).

The game was largely blown open by the Women's Lib movement and subsequent research into gender-comparative intelligence. It became an inescapable, official, scientific fact that all other things being equal, women are in general more intelligent. However, women still consistently underrate their IQs, while men consistently overrate theirs.

This oddity is encapsulated by Anita Loos' complaint: "The people I'm furious with are the women's liberationalists. They keep getting on soapboxes and proclaiming women are brighter than men. That's true, but it should be kept quiet or it ruins the whole racket."

Miss/Mrs/Ms

Women do not have a one-size-fits-all label to hang around their neck. 'Woman' sounds slightly biological and mature – not a word that a 16-year-old would readily apply to herself. 'Girl', which carries a hard-to-define sell-by date, is probably best avoided for any female over the age of eleven; although women of a certain age are permitted to use it of themselves and their chums, as in works' canteens, golf clubs and 'girls' night out'. 'Ladies' is for WCs, women in big hats, and women who are clearly anything but. One solution, widespread in America and Australia, is to use the word 'guys' irrespective of gender.

It annoys many women that their marital status has to be broadcast by the titles Miss and Mrs: they feel it should be nobody's business but their own. Besides, with more women keeping their own surname after marriage, it can be tricky to decide which title applies: as married women they are no longer Miss, but they are not Mrs Maiden Name either.

Ms has become the generally accepted compromise, but unfortunately no-one knows how to pronounce it without a faint sneer.

Feminism

It is tempting to assume that feminism has now become old hat – as outmoded as the hatpin and the mink stole with the head still on. This would be a great mistake, for along the way strewn with burnt bras there are plenty of embers which can easily be fanned into a fire.

The truth is that many women still feel hard done by, and there are lots of statistics to show that they get a raw deal. The women's movement was propelled forward by the French Revolution, the struggle for the emancipation of slaves, and votes for women, and plenty of women believe that there are more shackles to be torn asunder and that more heads should roll before the feminist goal of equality is reached.

At the base of feminism is a fundamental injustice, still unresolved. Eliana Gianini Belotti put it in a nutshell when she wrote: 'No woman, except for so-called deviants, seriously wishes to be male and have a penis. But most women would like to have the privileges and opportunities that go with it.'

But feminism can be a two-edged sword. Women are starting to miss the little courtesies that were once ingrained in men. There is a sad truth in the old chestnut which is brought out whenever men are accused of lack of politesse: "I offered my seat to a woman once and she turned out to be a feminist and shouted at me, so I'm scared to do it again." Someone must find this feminist harridan and stop her.

Women Drivers

There is a universal assumption that women and machines are simply incompatible. In fact it is really a question of attitude. Women do not wish to spend their Sunday afternoons dismantling their carburettor because (a) there are people they can pay do that for them, and (b) there are better things to do.

Society seems to have an in-built prejudice about this. It is perfectly acceptable for a man to say that he cannot make head or tail of the instructions for some mobile phone in a literal translation from Taiwanese; if a woman does the same, it is greeted by men with deep sighs and derision.

'Woman driver' is an insult generally flung by a man at a woman who drives like he does. But 90% of speeding convictions and 94% of accidents involve men, and insurance companies have responded by offering lower rates to women, as a better risk.

The assumption that women have no idea of what happens under the bonnet is also suspect: from sheer self-preservation, most women know how to spray spark plugs and change a tyre – but would rather pretend ignorance so as not to get oily.

Computers and videos come into the same category. It is true that more men than women explore the full potential of their computers, and that 85% of Internet users are men – but around the same percentage applies to the denizens of amusement arcades.

Many people are aware that Charles Babbage invented the first computer (almost all inventors are men*; women would rather solve the problems they already have), but bluffers could point out that it was a woman, Countess Ada Lovelace (daughter of Byron) who programmed it for him. And another, Commander Grace Hopper of the US Navy, who invented the programming language COBOL in the 1950s and, possibly more usefully, the term 'bug'.

Being Single

Unlike the bachelor, the word 'spinster' implies a crabby, lonely old age in a room ridden with cats and knick-knacks. Most single women prefer the term 'single woman' which they feel carries quite different connotations – debonair, carefree, and rather clever to have evaded the mundane chores of marriage. But

---

* So why is necessity the mother of invention, and not the father?

after 30, they may be viewed as either unnecessarily self-sufficient or rather daring (provided that they do not exude an air of quiet desperation).

To married men a single woman is a wasted asset. To women she is a loose cannon. The comment "she's never been married", usually made by married women to each other, is a form of put-down. For some, the single woman rests in limbo, her state and status similar to uncooked dough. Marriage is the oven of social pairing – living together in the microwave. Mere co-habiting is ruled out of this equation: she has not nailed her man.

Newsweek came up with the statistic that a college-educated woman of 30 had only a 20% chance of ever marrying; at 40, she had more chance of being murdered by a terrorist than finding a husband.

Despite the male fear of commitment, a random survey of people over 30 reveals that the vast majority of really bright men are married, and the vast majority of single women are really bright. Speculating about this in the company of married women requires care, but is nearly always successful with single ones.

Divorcees, by contrast, are seen as powerful – the mere fact of having been married proves they can fulfil woman's traditional role, and they are thereby freed to fulfil others. They have been there, done that, and come out stronger than ever on the other side.

Novelist Marie Corelli summed up her single state like this: "I never married because there was no need. I have three pets at home which answer the same purpose as a husband. I have a dog which growls every morning, a parrot which swears all the afternoon, and a cat that comes home late at night."

PMT/PMS

Women claim that they got dumped with periods because men couldn't take them. Not for nothing is it called 'the curse': periods are painful, smelly, messy and generally irksome. The only way to avoid menstruation is by becoming pregnant: out of the frying pan and into the fire.

Women's moods are controlled by this monthly cycle. Strange things happen to them as their period approaches – the phenomenon known as PMT. At least 50% of women say they suffer from it, and 5-10% to a debilitating degree. On their personal Richter scale, they may register anything from tremors of irritability to earth-shaking rages. (Why does it take six PMT women to change a light bulb? *Because it just DOES!!!*)

Tempers are not improved by the fact that they feel themselves to be distracted, clumsy, weepy, and heavier by several pounds. They may also get more interested in sex.

These days, there are endless products designed to make menstruation less burdensome – and from the advertisements, an unknowing man or child might assume that it was a time of unusual exuberance and flights of joy, accompanied by blue emissions.

Periods can be a trump card or a joker – a reassuring sign for some that they are not pregnant, devastating proof for others that they have again failed to conceive. Some women claim that their periods give them a sense of cyclical renewal, of physical cleansing. They may even remember their first period as a mystical experience that confirmed their entry into womanhood. But don't count on it.

Menopause

Women's attitude to the menopause is ambivalent. The natural cessation of fertility may have come in the past as a blessed relief to some but, today, women tend to regard it less as an end to problems associated with their periods, and more as an indication of new problems to come.

The diminution of female oestrogen is not, alas, an overnight process. It can involve:

– fatigue
– hot flushes or 'power surges'
– the onset of chin hair (associated with testosterone previously held in equilibrium by the oestrogen)
– inexplicable emotional outbursts
– loss of concentration of the kind that leads to buttering the cork mats instead of the toast.

To counteract this barrelful of woe, many women use Hormone Replacement Therapy (HRT), which effectively fools the body by replacing the lost oestrogen. (The Japanese who have the highest consumption of plant oestrogens, found in soya flour and linseed oil, have no word for the menopause.)

Humans are among the very rare animals to cease fertility in this way. It has been suggested that it serves a useful evolutionary function: women stop being burdened by having babies at a time when their own daughters are starting to produce them. This allows them to concentrate on handing down knowledge about breast feeding, potty-training, the best recipe for rabbit pie, the social acceptability of fish knives, and other tribal traditions.

To suggest that there is an equivalent 'male menopause' is greeted by most women with hoots of derision. They see this at best as an honorary title for the mid-life crisis. It certainly does not entail an equivalent physical or emotional see-saw.

Women can also have mid-life crises when they realise that they haven't had a life and are already half way through it. The idealism of youth may have vanished, but there may still be a last chance for fulfilment. This recognition hits women about ten years earlier than men – around the age of 35. As it happens, 35 is, for women, the average age for divorce.

Vulnerability

Women suffer from a deep sense of vulnerability. Part of this is purely physical – the fear of being raped, assaulted or just put upon by someone physically stronger and infinitely more aggressive. (In the US, 85% of violent crime is committed by men. The 15% committed by women may seem surprisingly high, but it includes domestic spats: when women murder, they usually kill someone they know.)

Fear defines a woman's freedom. She is simply unable to move around the world with the liberty of a man. A lone male hitchhiker is adventurous, a lone female one is 'looking for trouble'. Even in her own immediate neighbourhood she is subconsciously aware of the need to remain streetwise, check she is not being followed, be ever ready to flee or ask for help.

When a judge let a rapist go free because his mini-skirted victim had been 'asking for it', the American writer Ellen Cleghorn wryly remarked that the next time women saw an ugly man on the street they should shoot him: "After all, he knew he was ugly when he left the house. He was asking for it."

Ageing

A woman 'of a certain age' is still very reluctant to reveal it. The general view seems to be that she should pick a good age and stick with it, even if it technically illegitimises her offspring. Lying about age is a skill: it needs a facility for maths in order to calculate the year one was supposed to have been born, and care to ensure one did not start work at the tender age of ten. (However, the pendulum swings completely when a woman gets to 'a grand old age', and proudly announces that she is in her 79th/89th/99th year just to bask in the gasps of astonishment.)

Men reach the height of their fertility at around the age of 15, which in the case of a fair number of them happens to coincide with the end of their mental development. Women reach the height of their fertility in two waves, in the late teens, and again in their late thirties. This gives rise to a parallel paradox: aged around 15, girls do their utmost to look as though they are 35; when they are 35 they try in vain to look 15.

Women will make huge efforts to disguise the visible signs of ageing – dyeing their hair, slapping on creams, injecting fat into parts of their body which age has made thin and taking it out of parts grown too fat, and in many cases undergoing plastic surgery by winding in the whole skin covering like a sardine tin lid.

The real enemy is gravity: it makes women's bodies sag. If you look at women on a bus or train, the ones seated with stiff backs and rictus grins on their faces are probably engaged in pelvic floor exercises – designed to counteract the wearing effect of gravity on their internal organs.

The same gravitational effect on breasts is currently receiving attention from a group of aviation engineers who are working on designs for a truly effective bra. According to them, the problems of support for front-loaded mammary glands and engines mounted on the underside of aeroplane wings are, in engineering terms, identical.

Women, it must be emphasised, hide the effects of ageing in order to feel good about themselves. The fact that they might do it more if they are single and scanning the horizon for a decent man does not mean that women associate age with being less attractive to men. And the fact that men are pathetically attracted to young flesh is also entirely incidental. In female company, it is important to get this right.

Women know that men in any case – not that they are relevant here – actually prefer their women to grow old gracefully. The question is how to do it. What is easy enough at 39 is a matter of knife-edge judgement by 45: a little too much make-up, thigh, cleavage... And few woman would say, with the serene confidence of the actress Anna Magnani, "Please don't retouch my wrinkles. It took me so long to earn them."

12 WAYS TO ANNOY A WOMAN

1. Asking where something is before you've started to look.

2. Hovering at the door, looking repeatedly at your watch then, when she's ready, remembering something you have to do that will take half an hour.

3. Not listening with the appropriate amount of interest.

4. Giving her oven gloves for Christmas.

5. Being reluctant to accept invitations to go out; once out, being difficult to get back home again.

6. Saying "I didn't buy you chocolates because I thought you would say you were dieting."

7. Buying her the right garment in the right colour but the wrong size.

8. Telling her that *"We've* run out of toothpaste/peanut butter..."

9. Failing to notice that she's upset/changed her hair/revamped her wardrobe/lost seven pounds.

10. Getting on well with your mother; getting on even better with hers.

11. Leaving stubble in the basin.

12. Putting a fortnight's unsorted washing into the machine and turning everything pink.

12 THINGS A WOMAN HARDLY EVER SAYS TO A MAN

1. I think you're a wonderful driver.

2. Have a night out with your mates – you deserve it.

3. The dinner you cooked was so good I really *want* to wash everything in the kitchen – including the walls.

4. She has such a wonderful body – just like Pamela Anderson.

5. Honestly, rhinestones look just as good as diamonds.

6. I never expected you to remember, I know how busy you are.

7. My/your mother will understand totally if you aren't here. It's not every day there's a match.

8. You go ahead and enjoy yourself; I always prefer staying sober at parties.

9. Does my bum look too small in this?

10. No, let me – it's my round.

11. I adore hearing you snore.

12. You're right.

GLOSSARY

Ageing – Something that doesn't matter unless you are a cheese.

Ardent feminist – Woman whose real venom is reserved for women who take a different standpoint from her own.

Bra – An over shoulder boulder holder.

Breasts – Source of food for babies and fascination for men, also known as balloons, baps, bazoomas, boobs, bosoms, Bristols, bubs, bust, chubbies, dugs, fun bags, globes, grapefruits, kazongas, knockers, melons, tits, twin peaks, upper deck, wongas.

Childbirth – An experience likened to having one's lower lip pulled right up over one's head.

Clitoris – Female sex organ: the only bit of the human body (male or female) which appears to have no other function besides pleasure.

Doormat – Woman who allows her husband to wipe his feet on her, then shakes the mat outside and squares it off neatly.

Foreplay – Something men play at a few minutes before.

Friend – Bosom pal.

Housework – Things that no-one notices you have done but that everyone notices if you haven't.

Husband – Man who before marriage knows where his things are, and after it, doesn't.

Man's woman – Female with an inbuilt tracking device for seeking out the nearest male.

Menopause – Rather more than a pause between men.

Mother-in-law – The 'other woman' in a wife's life.

Oestrogen (spelt estrogen in the US and pronounced Eee-strogen in the UK) – The defining female hormone, also found in men.

PMT/PMS – Pre-menstrual tension (syndrome in the US, where everything is bigger). If you do not know what it is, try suggesting to a woman who has it that it's a figment of her imagination.

Pubic hair – The most visible aspect of female genitalia, a.k.a. bush, beaver, muff, Taz (Australian, after the shape of Tasmania), and according to some etymologists the origin of the word nitty-gritty.

Sexual harassment – The badgering and baiting of women by men, or in rare cases vice versa, in which case it is known as 'I've really got it made here!'

Testosterone – The defining male hormone, also found in women. Responsible for aggressive behaviour, hairiness and 'top-shelf' publications.

Tramp – Woman who distributes her favours too liberally a.k.a. bicycle, easy lay, jumper, slapper, scrubber, shag bag, tart (originally a diminutive of sweetheart).

Vagina/vulva – The passage through which all human life traditionally has passed, a.k.a. clunge, cockpit, conch, crack, cush, fanny (not in USA), front bottom, wick burner, happy valley, honey pot, prat, privy seal, pudenda, pussy, quim, tail, twat. There is also the hateful c.... word.

THE AUTHOR

Marina Muratore is child-care officer with years of experience working in nurseries in the public sector, a career which she feels has afforded her unique insight into the differences between men and women.

She is married to writer Antony Mason, author of *The Bluffer's Guide to Men* (and innumerable other great oeuvres). He sits upstairs, locked away with his important work, while she does the ironing and prepares the children's tea – for the child in the garden and the one upstairs.

Close collaboration on *The Bluffer's Guide to Women* has given Marina the chance to get even. Never before had they looked at men and women so thoroughly and so candidly – at least in each other's company. For her husband this process served to increase the fascinating mystery and mystique of women. For her, men became even more comprehensible, not to say transparent. As it happens, these were approximately the same relative positions that they started with.

THE BLUFFER'S GUIDES™

Available at £1.99* and £2.99:

Accountancy
Antiques
Astrology & Fortune Telling*
Ballet*
The Classics
Computers
Consultancy
Cricket
Doctoring
Economics
The European Union
The Flight Deck
Golf
The Internet
Journalism
Law
Management
Marketing
Men
Music
The Occult*

Opera
Personal Finance
Philosophy
Photography*
Public Relations
Public Speaking
The Quantum Universe
The Rock Business
Rugby
Science
Seduction
Sex
Skiing
Small Business
Stocks & Shares
Tax
Teaching
University
Whisky
Wine
Women

All these books are available at your local bookshop or newsagent, or by post or telephone from: B.B.C.S., P.O.Box 941, Hull HU1 3VQ. (24 hour Telephone Credit Card Line: 01482 224626)

Please add the following for postage charges: UK (& BFPO) Orders: £1.00 for the first book & 50p for each additional book up to a maximum of £2.50; Overseas (& Eire) Orders: £2.00 for the first book, £1.00 for the second & 50p for each additional book.